Lady Daphanny's Altar

Lady Daphanny's Altar

MY PRAYER FOR YOU TODAY IS...

DAPHANNY C. BAKER

J MERRILL

J Merrill Publishing, Inc.
434 Hillpine Drive
Columbus, OH 43207
www.JMerrill.pub

Library of Congress Control Number: 2023922760
ISBN-13: 978-1-961475-09-0 (Paperback)
ISBN-13: 978-1-961475-10-6 (eBook)

Book Title: Lady Daphanny's Altar
Author: Daphanny Baker

I dedicate this work to my previous First Lady.

I remember walking into New Jerusalem Church of God in Christ in Schweinfurt, GE, and her very words to me were, "God brought you here for me to pull some things out of you!"

By "things," she meant gifts, talents, and ministry. One Sunday morning, she asked me to lead prayer. I stated to her that I only prayed privately. Shortly after, she appointed me over the Prayer and Bible Band Circle. Hehe!

I'm grateful that she saw the prayer warrior in me even before I did, and she persisted in trying.
First Lady Martha E. Robinson

Introduction

I was taught earlier in life that I could make an altar anywhere I needed to. I didn't have to be in front of a crowd of pastors and elders, at church, or on exhibit. I could create an altar right in my living room, my office at work, or even at the wheel of my automobile.

I used this frequently—anytime I felt the need, I'd create a place to go before the Lord.

I have fashioned myself an altar to pray for daily life issues. My passion for people and their everyday dealings is intense.

"Lord, I beseech You on behalf of the conditions of my life; hear my humble cry."

Day One

MY PRAYER TODAY IS THAT YOU WILL TRUST GOD IN THE MIDST OF YOUR TEARS.

Crying is normal; let it all out and release. It does not mean that you don't trust God, nor does it mean that you are weak. Pain hurts, and it's okay to weep—but after you've done so, get up, get dressed, and keep going! God knows, and He has a plan. So, trust Him!

Day Two

MY PRAYER TODAY IS THAT WE LEARN HOW TO WAIT.

Trust God's timing. You—we—may not always like to wait, but timing is everything. Let's be real: if He gave you everything all at once, and you never had to wait for anything, how much would it be worth? "It's the wait that makes it worth it."

Day Three

MY PRAYER TODAY IS THAT WE'LL RECOGNIZE THAT EVERYTHING DONE WITH PURPOSE HAS A PURPOSE.

If the devil attacked you, it was on purpose—and if God didn't block it, there is a purpose. Romans 8:28 says, "And we know that all things work together for good to them that love God, to them who are the called according to his purpose."

Day Four

Just when I thought this was the time, God said, "Not yet." Delayed isn't denied, so I'll continue to wait on Him. I cannot preach to people, telling them to trust and wait, and then become weary and falter myself.

Jeremiah 29:11 assures us, "For I know the plans I have for you," declares the LORD, "plans to prosper you and not to harm you, plans to give you hope and a future."

So, since there's a plan in motion, I will stand still and wait on it, knowing that greater is coming.

Day Five

MY PRAYER TODAY IS THAT WE WILL GET IT TOGETHER.

Some people's mindset is that the devil has a hold of a person if they are addicted to drugs or alcohol, cursing, frequenting clubs, or promiscuity. But if one lacks self-control, gossips, lies, and harbors a terrible attitude, those are also the attributes of the devil. There's no big sin or little sin; murder isn't the only act that can prohibit one from entering Heaven.

Day Six

MY PRAYER TODAY IS THAT WE WILL YIELD AND NOT YELL.

When things irritate me, I see it as a sign that God has more work to do with me. I don't point the finger; I look directly at myself. This is when I need to retreat and pray. "Lord, I yield."

Day Seven

MY PRAYER TODAY IS THAT WE GAIN SOME SELF-CONTROL.

I'm learning to live in peace day by day—and you ought to take note. Stop giving everything your full attention, quit commenting on everything, and stop allowing people to live rent-free in your thoughts. Give it to God and rest in His wisdom. People will continue to control you if you let them. The quicker you sink to the lowest point, the more you permit yourself to do so. Begin waking up to realize that God is in charge of your life and that you control your decisions, period.

Day Eight

MY PRAYER TODAY IS THAT WE WILL TALK TO OURSELVES.

Day to day, I use my faith talk. "I will keep going. I will not become stagnant. I will live according to God's word. I will forgive and seek peace. I will be that example at my job. And I will love according to Christ's standards." They say you're crazy if you talk to yourself. I say, "You're crazy if you don't!" #FaithTalk #GetYouSome

Day Nine

MY PRAYER TODAY IS THAT GOD WILL
HEAL US THROUGH AND THROUGH.

We carry a tremendous amount of sorrow, pain, and disappointments with us every day. You don't realize how long you've been holding on to the pain until something triggers it. For us to effectively carry out our ministry, love our neighbors as ourselves, and pray for those who use us spitefully, we need God to heal us from the inside out.

Day Ten

I had to focus more on my own path and less on rescuing others when I began the journey of self-improvement. Initially, I tried to save myself while also helping others. It exhausted me! I must ensure I'm ready because it will be my number alone, not a shared one when my number is called. I understand some people won't make it. I can't become so engrossed in watching others and ensuring they live rightly that I neglect myself. It's God's role to judge others; my duty is to love, show love, and forgive. This is a personal matter.

Day Eleven

MY PRAYER TODAY IS THAT WE'LL BEGIN TO UTILIZE OUR TOOLS.

When life becomes weary, worship. When you feel powerless, pray. When problems arise, praise. When the cares of this life seem overwhelming, call on the name of God. There is a solution to the calamity of this world, and His name is Jesus. Try Him.

Day Twelve

MY PRAYER TODAY IS THAT I'M READY WHEN HE CALLS MY NAME.

Although spending the entire day in the spirit and speaking in tongues is not typical, I wish it were possible. It would be ideal if I had the final say—I wouldn't sin, I would never err, nothing would bother me. But truthfully, I aim to reach a point where I rely entirely on God and give thanks to Him before any conversation or planning because life is short, and my every endeavor is to make it into Heaven. #HelpMeLord

Day Thirteen

MY PRAYER TODAY IS THAT WE WILL EXHIBIT THE CHARACTERISTICS OF CHRIST.

I spoke with my neighbor today about their new dog, which they acquired a few weeks ago. "What is the dog's name?" my son asked. The neighbor replied they hadn't named the dog yet because they were still assessing his demeanor and character. Consider how many people observe you daily, trying to discern your identity and nature from your actions. Exercise extreme caution with your conduct, deeds, and character. In the end, you will be judged by the fruit you bear. Ultimately, the dog was named Monty, meaning "ruler."

Day Fourteen

MY PRAYER TODAY IS THAT YOU TURN IT OVER TO JESUS.

When you feel you're barely holding on and that you're walking alone, that's when God intervenes. When you reach the end of yourself, God can take over. Surrender it to Him. He can handle it much better.

Day Fifteen

MY PRAYER TODAY IS THAT WE WILL TAKE THIS WALK SERIOUSLY.

L ive as though you were walking hand in hand with Jesus. Would you speak as you do now? Would you act the same in secret? The Lord's eyes are everywhere. #HesWatching

Day Sixteen

MY PRAYER TODAY IS THAT YOU WOULD KEEP YOUR MARRIAGE SACRED.

Your spouse should always come first; there should never be room for anything else. When you decided to get married, the decision was made! Trying to merge two adults "as is" can be challenging, so you must not include any outside influences or pressures. Your spouse should be the one person who knows more about you than any friend, relative, or other individual. Three things make up a marriage: you, your partner, God, and nobody else. The end. #KeepItSacred

Day Seventeen

MY PRAYER TODAY IS THAT YOU WILL INTENSIFY YOUR COMMITMENT.

There is such a thing as happiness in marriage; however, you must be intentional with your spouse! I watched my daughter Diamond and her new husband take a moment for themselves tonight—it was beautiful. I guess it also helps if you like each other too, huh? #InvestInYourUnion

Day Eighteen

MY PRAYER TODAY IS THAT WE WILL LOOSE THE CHAINS.

Too many people choose to listen to someone who will agree with them rather than someone who can offer wise counsel. The truth sets you free, no matter how it makes you feel. Until you accept things as they are, you will remain bound. Have a donut if you want it sugar-coated!

Day Nineteen

MY PRAYER TODAY IS THAT WE KEEP OUR LOVE PURE.

Don't let what should be a great burning within turn out to be an ice-cold mess. Do not let sin taint your love.

Matthew 24:12 states, "And because iniquity shall abound, the love of many shall wax cold."

Day Twenty

MY PRAYER TODAY IS THAT WE'D BE MORE INTENTIONAL REGARDING OUR MATES.

Send a quick text or email if you have a moment! If you use that time for anything else, it shows your priorities and what really matters. When you were first in love, you would spend your entire break talking to your significant other and often return from break late. "I had a quick moment, so I was just checking on you," or "I'm excited to see you later," or "I wanted to hear your voice, so I called." Who still does this these days? #SomethingToThinkAbout

Day Twenty-One

MY PRAYER TODAY IS THAT YOU WILL
CHOOSE YOUR KING WISELY.

T raditionally, a king's role was to establish laws, maintain order, and make judgments in times of crisis. He was your "go-to guy!" The same holds true in marriage—if he is your king, he will initiate the changes you seek. He shouldn't be sidelined while you attempt to fix problems alone. A true king shows compassion and active involvement for those entrusted to him. You can relax when your king is truly "THE KING," knowing he's got it... because he's "That Guy!"

Day Twenty-Two

MY PRAYER TODAY IS THAT WE'D BECOME MINDFUL AND CONSIDERATE PEOPLE.

After enduring a terrible experience, you should be resolved not to inflict the same pain on others. Often, when someone is hurt, they pass that same pain on, forgetting how it made them feel initially. Be careful not to fall into the same vicious cycle! #GetStraightBeforeYouContaminate

Day Twenty-Three

MY PRAYER TODAY IS THAT WE'LL WALK AS WE TALK.

Proclaiming from the mountain that you've been saved and then living in opposition to all this noise you're making is the worst. Don't be that person! If you're not living it, don't broadcast it. Let your "no" be no, and your "yes" be yes.

Day Twenty-Four

MY PRAYER TODAY IS THAT WE WILL GO THROUGH WITH EASE.

We can all attest to enduring tough times on this journey called life. I may not have your story, but I sure have a story! I'm not naïve enough to think I'm the only one experiencing discomfort, nor should you be. One thing is certain: God will not put more on any of us than we can bear.

So, anchor up and ride the wave like a champion; you'll soon have a testimony to share and help someone else through!

Day Twenty-Five

MY PRAYER TODAY IS THAT WE'D TURN THINGS OVER TO GOD.

L isten, I'm at a point in my life where if it ain't about God (and yes, I said "ain't"), then I have little to no interest in it. I've stopped spending energy on arguments I can't win. I've adopted the motto, "I'm not arguing with anyone." This is the path to tranquility and sanity. Refuse to carry burdens that aren't yours and stop buying tickets to every show—you can't attend them all!

Day Twenty-Six

MY PRAYER TODAY IS THAT WE DON'T BECOME COMPLACENT.

In a matter of minutes, your life could change. Life isn't promised, and your life as it is isn't guaranteed. Anchor yourself in your relationship with the Lord—that's where your security lies.

Day Twenty-Seven

MY PRAYER TODAY IS THAT WE WILL
RENEW OUR MINDS.

Go down to the corner store and purchase a new mindset, set of rules, and a new pack of directions—the old ones are flawed and won't serve you well on this journey. I even had to update some of my equipment. Return complaining, worrying, and doubt. Replace them with assurance, faith, and a good posture. #YouWillGetThereFaster-WithoutBaggage

Day Twenty-Eight

MY PRAYER TODAY IS THAT YOU GRASP
THIS IMMEDIATELY:

It's crucial to want what's best for others! However, you must also want what's best for yourself.

Day Twenty-Nine

MY PRAYER TODAY IS FOR US TO BE FRUITFUL AND NOT BARREN.

Constantly evolving and not backpedaling. Speaking more wisely, acting more wisely, and making decisions you can be happy with rather than just feeling uneasy all the time. Life is short, and it's high time to stop the continual hesitation between two opinions (1 Kings 18:21). Live out what you speak about! Let your "yes" be yes, and your "no" be no (Matthew 5:37). Start living as the "you" that God intended you to be and not keep falling for the enemy's age-old deception. This condition is robbing, killing, and destroying you (John 10:10). #BeFruitfulNotBarren

Day Thirty

MY PRAYER TODAY IS THAT WE DON'T SQUANDER THE OPPORTUNITY TO BE GREAT.

Yesterday, I explained to a young person I work with that life is about living out your purpose, not just existing. You'll inevitably make mistakes but try not to let them consume your entire existence. I told her that if God took me at this moment, I'd be ready! Live your life so that, at the end, you can look back and say, "God has been good to me!"

I don't know about you, but I'm running hard for the finish line. I'm giving it everything I've got. No lazy living for me! I'm staying alert and in top condition. I refuse to be caught sleeping on duty—lecturing everyone about heaven and then missing out myself.

Day Thirty-One

MY PRAYER TODAY IS THAT WE REMAIN STEADFAST IN OUR FAITH.

Nothing is more disheartening to me than a man or woman of God who is weak. People today are so erratic and easily misled. They have no respect for the clergy. God is not pleased. Finding a credible leader who isn't exploiting their position is increasingly difficult. Urgently speaking, a great deal of suffering is being ignored because those in authority are simply looking the other way. No excuses will enter the gates. He didn't "just fall weak," and "she didn't just happen to be naked on the roof" 10 times out of 10. It was a setup! (Revelation 22:11-12)

Day Thirty-Two

MY PRAYER TODAY—AND TWO THINGS I'M WORKING ON...

My prayer today—and two things I'm working on—is not to take overthinking and this quick tongue into the new year. I'm learning to let things be, and people be people! (2 Corinthians 10:5) Casting down imaginations, and every high thing that exalts itself against the knowledge of God, and bringing into captivity every thought to the obedience of Christ; (James 1:19) Understand this, my dear brothers and sisters: You must all be quick to listen, slow to speak, and slow to anger. Slow down and let God have the last word.

Day Thirty-Three

MY PRAYER TODAY IS THAT PEOPLE WOULD MIND THEIR OWN BUSINESS.

If some individuals examined their own lives and choices, they wouldn't be so quick to judge and jump to conclusions about others. People often say, "If I were you," but they're not! And honestly, they have plenty of regrets just for being themselves! If they had begun with introspection, they wouldn't have had time to criticize you. Before you help another with their faults, take time to rectify your own. You might not have enough time to attend to theirs. #Busy #YourOwnHouse #CheckYourClosets

Day Thirty-Four

MY PRAYER TODAY IS THAT WE STOP CONDEMNING OURSELVES.

One Sunday, my husband delivered a sermon from Romans 5:8. He emphasized how God demonstrated His love for us: "In that, while we were still sinners, Christ died for us." I don't know what your "that" is that you think is so unforgivable, but I'm here to remind you that He already died for that... so forgive yourself and emerge renewed. He chose you while you were in the midst of it!

Day Thirty-Five

MY PRAYER TODAY IS THAT GOD WILL
BESTOW UPON US A PEACE BEYOND OUR
OWN UNDERSTANDING.

Release us, Oh God, from the confines of our minds. Amen.

(Philippians 4:7) And the peace of God, which surpasses all understanding, will guard your hearts and minds through Christ Jesus.

Day Thirty-Six

MY PRAYER TODAY IS THAT I WOULD PLEASE GOD INTIMATELY.

By keeping all His commandments and pursuing the things He loves—a cheerful giver, treating people well, forgiving others, and loving one another. I'm so grateful that He chose me—that it's essential for me to show Him.

(1 Samuel 13:14) But now your kingdom will not continue. The Lord has sought for Himself a man after His own heart, and the Lord has commanded him to be commander over His people, because you have not kept what the Lord commanded you.

Day Thirty-Seven

MY PRAYER TODAY IS THAT MY HEART IS CLEAN AND FREE OF DEBRIS.

There's a song by Donnie McClurkin that says, "Search me, Lord." Shine the light from heaven on my soul. If you find anything that shouldn't be, take it out and strengthen me. 'Cause I wanna be right, I wanna be saved, and I wanna be whole.

My innermost desire is to operate daily in God's divine love with a clean and pure heart.

(Psalm 51:10) Create in me a clean heart, O God, and renew a steadfast spirit within me.

Day Thirty-Eight

MY PRAYER TODAY IS THAT I WON'T COMPLAIN BUT TRUST GOD.

I'm learning to put this into practice, as well as trusting God in every situation.

Proverbs 3:5-6 says,

"Trust in the Lord with all your heart, and lean not on your own understanding; in all your ways acknowledge Him, and He shall direct your paths."

God knows the direction we're going in; allow Him to lead.

Day Thirty-Nine

MY PRAYER TODAY IS THAT I WILL CONTINUE TO TRUST HIM "IN THE WAIT."

There's a difference between "just waiting" and waiting while BELIEVING that God will deliver you from the wiles of the enemy and trusting Him to restore what the enemy stole when all hope seems lost. It's in HOW you wait.

Job 14:14 asks,

"If a man dies, shall he live again? All the days of my service I would wait, till my renewal should come."

Waiting won't kill you! Trust God amid your greatest trials, KNOWING that He will make everything well.

Day Forty

MY PRAYER TODAY IS THAT I WILL NOT ALLOW THINGS THAT SHOULD NOT LINGER TO LINGER BUT WILL USE MY GOD-GIVEN AUTHORITY TO COMMAND THAT THEY DISSIPATE.

Sometimes, we must take direct authority in the spiritual realm to speak those things out of our way.

Jesus said, "Whoever says to this mountain, 'Be removed and be cast into the sea,' and does not doubt in his heart, but believes that those things he says will be done, he will have whatever he says" (Mark 11:23).

Keep nothing that will hinder your walk! Demand that it MOVE, and you walk accordingly.

Day Forty-One
MY PRAYER TODAY IS:

God, USE ME for Your glory! Any unused area, use it! Any area that is dead, wake it up! I completely avail myself to walk in every charge, every mission, and everything that You've assigned to my hands in THIS season! In Jesus' Name, Amen.

Ezekiel 36:26 states,

"I will give you a new heart and put a new spirit within you; I will take the heart of stone out of your flesh and give you a heart of flesh."

Operate in the greater call!

Day Forty-Two

MY PRAYER TODAY IS:

My prayer today is that God will restore to me the days before all the hurt, betrayal, denial, and disappointments and give me a "POST" service that pleases, edifies, and magnifies You, God! Use that unused portion of me! My desire is to serve as though I was never hurt.

Psalm 61:1-2 reads,

"Hear my cry, O God; listen to my prayer. From the ends of the earth I call to you, I call as my heart grows faint; lead me to the rock that is higher than I."

#BetterNotBitter

Day Forty-Three

MY PRAYER TODAY IS THAT WE'LL
RECOGNIZE THAT EVERYTHING DONE
WITH PURPOSE HAS A PURPOSE.

If the devil hit you, it WAS on purpose... and if God didn't block it, there IS a PURPOSE!

See Romans 8:37.

Day Forty-Four

IN MY PRAYER THIS MORNING:

My revelation was that we, as saints, must anoint and keep those areas of our homes sacred. Anoint your head, your body, your bed/sheets, doorposts, mailboxes, and even your cell phones. There are so many areas that the enemy wants to infiltrate. We must keep watch and guard those areas diligently because the enemy wants to use any door to distract us.

Psalm 119:2-5 states, "Blessed are those who keep his statutes and seek him with all their heart; they do no wrong but follow his ways. You have laid down precepts that are to be fully obeyed. Oh, that my ways were steadfast in obeying your decrees!"

Day Forty-Five

To REACT like Jesus! That is my every endeavor. Even though life seems rough, God, I still trust You to see us through!

Psalm 23:4 comforts, "Yea, though I walk through the valley of the shadow of death, I will fear no evil: for thou art with me; thy rod and thy staff they comfort me."

Day Forty-Six

MY PRAYER TODAY IS...

L ord, help me stay the course. Keep my mind steadfast forevermore! Amen.

Galatians 6:9 (MSG) reminds us, "So let's not allow ourselves to get fatigued doing good. At the right time we will harvest a good crop if we don't give up or quit. Right now, therefore, every time we get the chance, let us work for the benefit of all, starting with the people closest to us in the community of faith."

Day Forty-Seven

MY PRAYER TODAY IS THAT THE LORD WOULD BLOT OUT MY TRANSGRESSIONS.

In today's world, my every endeavor is to hear the voice of the Lord and act accordingly. I don't just want Him to use me; I want Him to use the yielded, clean version of me. I want to operate in love, forgiveness, and purity of heart.

Psalm 51:1 implores, "Have mercy upon me, O God, according to thy lovingkindness: according unto the multitude of thy tender mercies blot out my transgressions."

Day Forty-Eight

MY PRAYER TODAY IS THAT YOU'D HEAL ME FROM THE INSIDE OUT.

Help me to forgive and extend pardon to each person who has hurt me and sinned against You, God, in trying to reach me. Help me not to be like the unmerciful servant (Matthew 18:21-35). Let Your word convict me EVERY TIME! Continue to let me receive the word that You've sent to me through Your messengers; never allow me to turn a deaf ear to it.

Psalm 119:11 declares, "Thy word have I hid in mine heart, that I might not sin against thee."

Day Forty-Nine

MY PRAYER TODAY IS:

G od, help me see You in all things; never let me lose sight of Your path for me. Let YOUR WORD resonate in me every time.

Psalm 119:105 enlightens, "Thy word is a lamp unto my feet, and a light unto my path."

Day Fifty

MY PRAYER TODAY IS:

I remind myself to put You first, God—Your will for me, Your way for me, Your plan for me.

Matthew 6:33 (KJV) tells us, "But seek ye first the kingdom of God, and his righteousness; and all these things shall be added unto you."

Day Fifty-One

MY PRAYER TODAY IS THAT WE KEEP OUR VOWS.

While eating on my lunch break today, I dropped a piece of chicken in my car. I scrambled for it because I didn't want it left there. Backstory: I had been working so much that I hadn't had time to clean my car, and anyone who knows me knows I don't like even the smallest piece of paper in my car. So, on Monday, I cleaned my car from top to bottom and vowed not to let it get dirty again. The moral of the story is never to judge the urgency of someone's fire for God because you don't know the dirt they vowed never to return to.

Day Fifty-Two

MY PRAYER TODAY IS THAT GOD WILL
GIVE ME CONTINUAL DAILY BREAD TO
SUSTAIN ME THROUGHOUT THE DAY
AND THAT I WILL SHARE WITH OTHERS
AS THE HOLY SPIRIT SHARES WITH ME.

In this busy world, so much is missed because of the various happenings, the loud noise, and all the clutter. My endeavor is to share with others, even in the midst of everything.

Day Fifty-Three

MY PRAYER TODAY IS THAT WE MIMIC
CHRIST—OUR ACTIONS, REACTIONS,
LOVE, WALK, TALK, ETC., "CHRIST!"

Genesis 1:26 (KJV) says, "And God said, Let us make man in our image, after our likeness."

Day Fifty-Four

MY PRAYER TODAY IS THAT WE EXEMPLIFY LOVE!

Love is patient, kind, considerate, and true. Love is being loving when you don't feel like it. Love is that kiss every morning, even when at odds. Love is missing her when you're away and can't wait to get home at the end of the day. Love is ensuring she's alright and assuring her that she's protected. Love is her confidence that she has your attention, conversation, and love. Love is your dependability when times are hard. Love is undoubtedly knowing that she can trust you with her life. I love Love! 🤍

"Let everything you do be done in love." (1 Corinthians 16:14, AMP)

Day Fifty-Five

MY PRAYER IS THAT I DO RIGHT, EVEN IF OTHERS DO WRONG.

When God called me to ministry, I told Him I didn't want to be mediocre. And every time I ask Him why He lets others get away with wrong and yet convicts me every time I even look like I'm veering to the left, He reminds me I said I didn't want to be like everyone else. When I'm mistreated and unable to respond, it hurts, but I'm soon reminded that Christ was more than mistreated, yet without sin. "That I may know Him!" is more important. "Vengeance is mine, saith the Lord." Instead of attempting to retaliate, reactivate your declaration. (Proverbs 15:3, AMP) says, "The eyes of the Lord are in every place, watching the evil and the good."

Day Fifty-Six

MY PRAYER TODAY IS THAT WE ALL THRIVE.

There's more than enough room for all of us to thrive. No one can be me but me, and no one can be you but you. We all have something we are destined to do. So, let's encourage one another and rise up!

Day Fifty-Seven

MY PRAYER IS THAT WE KEEP GOING.

Sometimes, you're unsure what God's plan is for you, but believe me, He is the expert. When you're ready to give up, He sends a little sanctified reminder to keep going. I was there yesterday, and naturally, God sent a reminder of the importance of "to the kingdom!" Just a note: You may not always want to do what is instructed but hold on. It will all make sense in the end.

Day Fifty-Eight

MY PRAYER TODAY IS THAT WE WON'T
LET THE ENEMY TRICK US OUT OF OUR
CREDIBILITY.

Being credible is essential when you speak. People need to trust what you do and say. (Proverbs 11:3 NLT) states, "Honesty guides good people; dishonesty destroys treacherous people."

Day Fifty-Nine

MY PRAYER TODAY IS THAT WE BECOME
HELPERS TO ONE ANOTHER.

Many people think the glory is in bragging. Nope, the glory is in testifying! Don't just tell me you made it; tell me how you got there!

Day Sixty

MY PRAYER TODAY IS... GOD, HELP YOUR
PEOPLE.

This is a different batch of people nowadays.

#DifferentSaints (not dedicated)
#DifferentSpouses (not faithful)
#DifferentFriends (not loyal)
#DifferentChildren (not respectful)
#DifferentNeighbors (not loving)
#DifferentPastors (not Christ-like)

God, help us live life as You've instructed.

Day Sixty-One

MY PRAYER TODAY IS THAT WE'D HOLD ON.

Things may not be as you'd like, and it may seem like a road of never-ending turmoil but continue to trust God. I know the feeling, but what I am sure of is that this is only temporary. God is faithful to His word—rest assured, He will come through for you.

Day Sixty-Two

MY PRAYER TODAY IS THAT WHEN WE
RECEIVE BAD NEWS, WE WILL
IMMEDIATELY PRAY TO ALLOW GOD TO
BLOCK ALL DOUBT AND FEAR.

God, I believe YOU, not the news!

1 Thessalonians 5:17-18 (KJV) says, "Pray without ceasing. In every thing give thanks: for this is the will of God in Christ Jesus concerning you."

Day Sixty-Three

MY PRAYER TODAY IS, LORD, HELP US HELP OTHERS.

It's so hard to find a married couple that others can glean from nowadays because everyone wants to appear as though their marriage is perfect. So many cry inside or walk away because they have no one to turn to. Do you mean you never disagree? You mean you've never slept on the couch? You mean you've never wanted to leave? Some marriages could be saved "if" some of these "perfect" couples would share how they manage to be "so perfect." I endeavor to share with other couples the few things that work for me. I don't have all the answers, but I don't mind sharing the nuggets I know if it will help save marriages.

#LifeLineSent

Day Sixty-Four

MY PRAYER TODAY IS THAT WE LEARN TO
FORGIVE QUICKLY.

I often say that forgiveness is usually for your benefit, not for others. You don't wake up saying, "I'm going to forgive someone to please them"—you forgive to please God and to live in peace. I'm also learning not to get caught up watching others on this journey; they may never change! And frankly, it's my journey, not theirs. It's intentional for me. Don't be discouraged by the hiccups along the way; keep going and striving. The enemy will use distractions to get you off track but keep your eyes on the prize. Let your progress thus far be your motivation. Don't give up because of one or two setbacks.

Day Sixty-Five

MY PRAYER TODAY IS THAT WE LIVE LIVES THAT ARE WORTHWHILE.

Respect is at an all-time low nowadays. It used to be that folks could leave their doors open without fear of intrusion. I recall when people would respect churches, even from the outside. These days, you might see people smoking, drinking, and swearing on church steps. Once-covert marital infidelity is now done openly and thoughtlessly. The younger generation now treats everyone equally, unlike previous generations, who respected their elders. We are in the last days when, as the Bible says, "the love of many shall wax cold" (Matthew 24:12, KJV). People have lost respect for others' lives, belongings, and feelings. These are sad times, but the remnant must uphold the standard.

Day Sixty-Six

MY PRAYER TODAY IS THAT WE CONTINUE TO PRAY FOR ONE ANOTHER.

We are all dealing with life's challenges. My struggle might not be as difficult as yours, and vice versa, but neither should be dismissed or underestimated. Let's keep each other in constant prayer. You never know who might need it.

Day Sixty-Seven

IN PRAYER TODAY, THE QUESTION IS,
"WHAT'S WRONG WITH IT?"

What's wrong with apologizing even when you're not at fault, and what's wrong with falling in love again after being hurt? What's wrong with holding your tongue when you think you should speak up, and what's wrong with forgiving a major offense? What's wrong with maintaining order amidst chaos and praying for those who have wronged you or are wronging you? The answer is—nothing! Many people are performing wrong; we want tit-for-tat to repay evil with evil. However, what's wrong with overcoming evil with good? Satan's tactics are ripe in life; why not set a good example for him? There's nothing wrong with that.

#StandDifferent

Day Sixty-Eight

MY PRAYER TODAY IS THAT WE WON'T JUST GO WITH THE FLOW.

What do we do with the devil's schemes? We combat them with God's word! "I am more than a conqueror, and I can overcome any obstacle through Christ. We are healed by His stripes, and He will never forsake us." We don't just absorb what the enemy throws at us; we block and counterstrike. Just because something forms doesn't mean it has to thrive, and just because something appears to be doesn't mean it will be. Yesterday, I received some news but didn't really "receive" it. God is greater than any news, analysis, judgment, or obfuscation. Ultimately, God has the final say, and I believe God!

#ByHisStripes #ItsAccordingToYourFaith

Day Sixty-Nine

MY PRAYER TODAY IS THAT YOU REMAIN IN THE FLOW.

Our minds can sometimes be like a conveyor belt, constantly moving, adding new items as soon as one is dealt with. Let the belt keep moving. Address what you can and let go of what you can't. Give it your best shot, then move on to the next issue, for life is too short to dwell on the unsolvable.

#KeepItPushing #LifeIsHealthierThatWay

Day Seventy

MY PRAYER TODAY IS THAT WE POSSESS AN ATTITUDE OF GRATITUDE.

As I go about my day, I can't help but give thanks to God for all He is doing in my life. Gratitude is the attitude to have; it's the posture to receive all of God's choice blessings. I thank God daily for choosing me to carry His mantle, for allowing me to birth children who will bring forth His fruit, and for entrusting me with a ministry that will honor Him.

I'm so grateful!

Day Seventy-One

MY PRAYER TODAY IS THAT YOU'LL LIVE YOUR LIFE WITH INTENTION.

Life is full of possibilities. It's possible to succeed, travel, see the world, and start over when life has let you down. As long as you're breathing, you can do something possible! Don't give up. Keep going. Start over a million times if you must. Tomorrow is not promised, but if you're granted a new day, take it as a chance to keep living. Many people may plan to end their lives. You decide to live yours.

Day Seventy-Two

MY PRAYER TODAY IS THAT YOU FOLLOW YOUR OWN PATH.

There's life in living and true happiness in declaring "I'm happy." We must see the value of important things and recognize the veritable treasures within them. Lately, the brevity of life has become very real to me. I'm learning, even now, to let God be God in my affairs while I devote myself to His work. Sometimes, we need to relearn things, or we just need a reminder. I'm also learning that listening to everyone's opinion isn't always the best. We must follow the path designed specifically for us. We get off course by following the wrong guides. The Creator will lead you to all truth, and that's where life and happiness lie.

#BeHappy

Day Seventy-Three

MY PRAYER TODAY IS THAT CHRIST IS THE CENTER.

I am tired of the same old nonsense. "You'll get tired when you're truly tired," a wise woman once said. I have reached that point. I'm weary of the same paths, follies, and actions with no progress or glory to God. We should strive to please God in all we do; therefore, we must act in ways that honor Him. Now is the perfect time to embark on a new, mature, Christ-centered path, convinced that if God isn't the center, I want no part of it! #GetTired

Day Seventy-Four

MY PRAYER TODAY IS THAT WE PAY ATTENTION.

When has a relationship run its course? When do you decide enough is enough? It's when people stop listening, other things take priority, or your concerns are dismissed as "nonsense" or trivial. What matters to you should matter to them. Never let someone who lacks understanding dismiss your concerns by pretending to be wise. Even if relationships are challenging, they're unattainable without genuine effort. I refuse to stay where I'm unproductive and stagnant, and I won't shout at those who aren't listening. Know when to walk away! Be discerning. Know when to hold on and when to let go.

Day Seventy-Five

MY PRAYER TODAY IS THAT YOU DENOUNCE THE HEAVINESS.

What is your sunken place? Your city, job, home, church? Do you enter a place and feel overwhelmed, as if you can't see through the fog? It's not the place itself—there's something you need to confront and pray over. Don't write off the entire place; once you identify and address the root cause, you may find joy there again.

Day Seventy-Six

MY PRAYER TODAY IS THAT YOU KEEP YOUR SONG.

Where did my song go? Suddenly, the volume lowered, and I found myself in silence, giving the enemy my undivided attention to distract and deter me. God gave me a song in the womb to sustain me, but when I don't listen to it, I'm vulnerable. Today, I turned on the radio, and my song drowned out the noise attacking my spirit. My music will disrupt the viruses and diseases that aim to impair my communication with God. Thank You, God, for my song, and forgive me for ever turning it down.

Day Seventy-Seven

MY PRAYER IS THAT WE FOCUS ON OUR OWN SOUL'S SALVATION.

Do you know people who think every move you make is about them? You're not that important! They believe if you're in their vicinity, you must be stalking them, or if you have something similar, you're copying them. Blessings come from God! My life isn't consumed with others' lives. People can be vain, believing you're wrapped up in their affairs. Life is too short for that—we're too busy living for Jesus. Tell them to do the same!

Day Seventy-Eight

MY PRAYER IS THAT MARRIED COUPLES
STAY MARRIED.

Married couples need to date each other! Add some fun, some "sexy" to it. Saying "I do" is where the genuine work begins. Devote time to your relationship—work on it, and there'll be less infidelity and fewer divorces. Focus on your own affairs. #WorkOnYourOwnYard

Day Seventy-Nine

MY PRAYER TODAY IS THAT YOU ALLOW GOD TO DO THE EDITING.

P eople invest so much in your life without contributing anything tangible. Do not let their opinions or advice disrupt your journey. Your life is yours to live, and God knows the path you should take. Let others keep their opinions to themselves.

Day Eighty

MY PRAYER TODAY IS THAT I CONTINUE TO GIVE THANKS.

Since my name isn't in the obituary, I have another chance to thank God! He is amazing, and we should use every breath to thank Him for His love, grace, and protection. We received many blessings we didn't deserve, yet He still found us worthy. Reflect on this and thank Him for it.

Psalm 107:1-2 (KJV) says, "O give thanks unto the Lord, for he is good: for his mercy endureth forever. Let the redeemed of the Lord say so, whom he hath redeemed from the hand of the enemy."

Day Eighty-One

MY PRAYER TODAY IS THAT WE TESTIFY.

What's your testimony? Survive a car accident? Spared by a stray bullet? Left an abusive relationship? Has God healed your marriage, kept a loved one alive, or helped you overcome addiction? Are you using your story to help others? Just saying, "He did it for me," can impact many lives. By sharing that you made it, someone else may realize they can, too. Share your story and inspire others to overcome!

Day Eighty-Two
MY PRAYER TODAY IS THAT WE MAKE WISE CHOICES.

Your current situation is the result of past choices. The decisions you make today define your future.

#ChooseWisely

Day Eighty-Three

MY PRAYER TODAY IS THAT WE'LL DIE TO THE FLESH.

You don't truly know how to live until you learn to die to the flesh. #KillTheFlesh

Day Eighty-Four

MY PRAYER TODAY IS THAT WE
CONTINUE TO EVOLVE.

S easons change, people change, designs change —so should you. Each new day is an opportunity for improvement. Resolve to be a better version of yourself than you were yesterday. Be kind to yourself. Treat yourself well. Aim high and decide nothing will stand in your way. You have yet to realize your full potential.

Day Eighty-Five

MY PRAYER TODAY IS THAT WE LEARN TO FOLLOW JESUS.

P eople may often label you weak because your choices do not align with their views. Yet, as you take a leap of faith in adversity, God proudly says, "Look at the strength of my child." Even you, blindly following God's guidance, might not understand your well-directed steps. But the outcome is splendid when you adhere to your divine blueprint. Some actions and places could have led to different results if we had paused, taken a seat, closed our mouths, and turned to our Father. Trust in the Lord's direction, not the devil's snares—Daddy knows best!

Day Eighty-Six

MY PRAYER TODAY IS THAT WE FOCUS ON WHERE WE ARE GOING.

What constitutes a grand life? Is it money, fancy cars, a big house, a company, or education? For me, it's the assurance of entry. Material possessions have taken a backseat because life is so fleeting these days. There's nothing subtle about the pandemic—get your affairs in order! Sleep peacefully, knowing you can't take material possessions with you. Focus not on the temporal but on the eternal. #LifeIsShortThenYouDie

Day Eighty-Seven

MY PRAYER TODAY IS THAT WE REALIZE NO ONE IS PERFECT.

What are the origins of relationship and friendship values? Did they start when the thief on the cross asked Jesus to remember him, from Judas's betrayal, or when Eve tempted Adam into committing a significant sin? This shows us no relationship is flawless, regardless of origin or development. Yet we are instructed to forgive. I am not saying you must continue the relationship, but I am saying everyone makes mistakes. Remember this when you consider saying "yes."

#NoOneIsPerfect

Day Eighty-Eight

MY PRAYER TODAY IS THAT WE KEEP
GOD AS THE AUTHOR AND THE
FINISHER.

Never give someone control over your dreams and aspirations, as your success or failure would be in their hands.

Day Eighty-Nine

MY PRAYER TODAY IS THAT WE LIVE OUR OWN LIVES.

A revelation jolted me awake this morning: Never base your relationship on what you assume is happening in someone else's home. As a child, I saw my adopted dad as the sole provider, forgetting my adopted mom owned a restaurant. What worked for them might not work for you. Whether it's dual incomes or a stay-at-home mom, do it your way, not the Joneses' way.

Day Ninety

MY PRAYER TODAY IS THAT WE WON'T
ALLOW THINGS, OTHERS' OPINIONS, OR
EVEN OUR OWN DOUBTS TO OBSTRUCT
WHAT GOD HAS ORDAINED.

You might not get it right the first or second time but keep pressing on with God, and eventually, you will. Do not waver or wander. Your steps are ordered—just walk it out.

Psalm 37:23 (KJV) states, "The steps of a good man are ordered by the LORD: and he delighteth in his way."

Day Ninety-One

MY PRAYER TODAY IS THAT WE'D HOLD ON.

When you're holding on for dear life as challenges assault you from every direction, continue to hold on. You may feel your grip weakening, but do not let go. God knows how much you can bear and will keep you from falling. Keep your gaze fixed on the prize; He will not fail you. #HoldOn

Day Ninety-Two

MY PRAYER TODAY IS THAT WE KEEP PUSHING.

As Christians, we are called to emulate Christ's example. Sometimes, you feel overwhelmed, but that's when you hand it over to God. Turn on worship music, delve into Scripture, and pray! Preserve your joy and witness from the adversary's taint. We know the devil's job, but are we doing ours? Follow Christ—your steps are preordained.

Day Ninety-Three

MY PRAYER IS THAT WE KEEP THE MAIN THING THE MAIN THING.

The devil thinks he can compromise your core by meddling with your marriage, finances, or children. When you focus on these distractions, you lose sight of what's truly important. He thought that afflicting Job would make Job curse God, but because Job remained steadfast, he was abundantly blessed. #KeepYourEyesOnYourCore

Day Ninety-Four

MY PRAYER TODAY IS THAT WE'D TAKE OUR OWN ADVICE.

H ave you ever preached to others or your children only to find yourself drinking from the same cup of words? You've advocated for wise choices, good stewardship, trusting in God, and accepting His will. Whenever I want to act impulsively, my children remind me of my declaration. We must heed our own advice, as vows are made to be kept.

Ecclesiastes 5:5 (KJV) advises, "Better is it that thou shouldest not vow, than that thou shouldest vow and not pay."

Day Ninety-Five

MY PRAYER TODAY IS THAT WE TRUST HIS PLAN.

Ever wonder why things can't go as you planned? You want perfection, or at least a livable situation; you've mapped things out since your youth, but somehow, things are not progressing as projected. Though we acknowledge God's ways and thoughts are not ours, we implore Him to heed our requests. We must have faith that God's will prevails and that all things work together for good for those who are called according to His purpose.

#It'sHisPurpose #It'sHisPlan #It'sHisPath

Day Ninety-Six

MY PRAYER TODAY IS THAT WE LET GOD
BE THE DECIDING FACTOR, NOT MAN.

We make decisions throughout life, and we often look back to gauge others' reactions for reasons unknown even to us. At some point, we must decide for ourselves, not worrying about others' opinions. You're left alone with your choices, good or bad. I've realized I won't base decisions on others anymore, nor will I concern myself with their opinions. While people live their lives, we must live ours. Be free from the weight of others' judgments. Live your life!

#BeFree #LiveYourLife

Day Ninety-Seven

MY PRAYER TODAY IS THAT I WILL CONTINUE WITH CLASS.

No matter what is said or done, I resolve to carry on. Determined to stay on course, I remain classy despite adversity and contentious encounters. I have firmly approached things differently than I have in the past. Through it all, I will persevere with dignity and class.

Day Ninety-Eight

MY PRAYER TODAY IS THAT MARRIED
PEOPLE WILL PUT IN THE WORK.

Relationships are not always as we portray them. In public, we may boast about our partners and pretend all is well, but often, things are amiss behind closed doors. Unfulfillment, lack of support, voids, and absence of intimacy can lurk beneath the surface. Yet, we declare, "That's my Boo!" I notice people seeking validation through online flirtations when that connection could be kindled with their partner if only they put in the effort. Relationships require work—stop neglecting each other. Flirt with your own mate, invest in each other, and resolve conflicts. Do the work to make it genuine so you won't need to maintain a facade.

Day Ninety-Nine

MY PRAYER TODAY IS THAT IT TURNS OUT TO BE A GREAT DAY.

What does your internal weather forecast predict? A beautiful sunny day, rain, a storm advisory, a tornado warning, or should we brace for a hurricane? Remember, the weatherman can be wrong. Despite a forecast of rain, the sun might shine through, especially here in Pennsylvania. Do not let a gloomy prediction set the tone for your day. Even if it must rain, learn to dance in it. Be prepared for the not-so-good days; when you know challenges are ahead, brace yourself and dress for the occasion. Life is what you make it—set your own forecast.

Day One Hundred

MY PRAYER TODAY IS THAT WE BECOME DRIVEN.

What motivates you? What keeps you going, positive or negative? A negative drive can be a powerful motivator—it's where I excel. I earned my degree against the odds and have thrived in challenging environments. Let whatever drives you be a force for prosperity and help you overcome the hurdles meant to trip you up. A bit of motivation can do wonders.

About the Author

Daphanny Denette C. Baker, a native of Plant City, Florida, and raised in Newark, New Jersey, by the late Clifford A. Porter and Alean R. Porter, has served in various capacities in the church since her salvation at the tender age of 15.

A graduate of Ewing High School and a licensed Cosmetologist, she holds a Bachelor's in Criminal Justice and an MBA.

In 1999, she answered her call to ministry and was licensed as an Evangelist Missionary in the Church of God in Christ. Lady Baker loves the Lord and dedicates much of her time to helping those in pain.

She is married to Bishop Melvin T. Baker. She is the mother of four beautiful children—Eryonna, Reyc'haun, Diamond, and Javier—and grandmother to Ani'yah Reyana.

 facebook.com/daphanny.baker

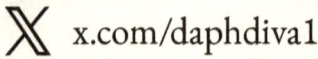 x.com/daphdiva1

instagram.com/daphannycrump

Also by
Daphanny C. Baker

365 Days of Transparency

Back Cover

Prayer is an act of invocation or deliberate communication designed to connect with our Savior. Sincere prayer can actualize God's promises, and those devoted to prayer vigilantly guard against the devil's wiles. Committed to standing on Nehemiah's wall, I hope my persistence in praying for God's people and their needs will bear fruit.